RILEY HUNTER

The Ultimate Guide to Las Vegas for $30 or Less

A Budget Traveler's Guide to the Best of the Strip: Take the Gamble out of your Vegas Experience

Contents

1

Introduction

Welcome to the Ultimate Guide to Las Vegas Activities for $30 or Less. My name is Riley Hunter and I am extremely excited to write this book. You see, my husband and I visit Las Vegas a lot. We love Las Vegas and we love to gamble but sometimes the casinos don't love us back. That bankroll we bring with us in hopes of it growing, multiplying and sustaining us for the entirety of our trip, well, let's just say sometimes we find ourselves enjoying the view from our room sooner than we would have liked.

Like most people when we thought of Las Vegas, images of flashing neon lights, busy casinos, and high-stakes gambling instantly came to mind. We soon learned that we needed to explore some other parts of Las Vegas if this was some place we could enjoy coming to for years to come. We needed to explore another side of Las Vegas and no not the OTHER side of Vegas that you can't talk about when you leave. We wanted to explore the family friendly side of Vegas that you can't wait to get home and tell your friends and family about.

We learned that Las Vegas is a city that offers budget-friendly activities that will provide more of a guaranteed return on investment than any sports book wager we could place. Oh yes, beyond the slot machines and poker tables, there's a vibrant city brimming with unique, free or budget-friendly adventures waiting to be discovered.

This book is your ultimate guide to uncovering the cheap and free treasures of Las Vegas. Whether you are a frequent Vegas visitor or its your first-time, you'll find more than enough activities that cost $30 or less, ensuring you have an unforgettable experience without the huge price tag.

From exploring the iconic Las Vegas Strip to enjoying free entertainment and discovering budget-friendly dining options, this guide will help you navigate the strip like a pro. You'll find tips on outdoor adventures, shopping, and insider tricks to make the most of your trip. Our focus is on experiences that won't break the bank, particularly during the vibrant late spring and summer seasons.

Las Vegas is more than just a gambler's paradise. It's a city full of surprises, waiting to be explored. So, grab your sunscreen and walking shoes—let's uncover the magic of the Las Vegas strip and surrounding area, one budget-friendly adventure at a time.

2

On the Strip

Walking Tours

Many people find walking tours both educational and engaging. These tours reveal insights about the city and the Vegas Strip that glitzy commercials often overlook. Walking tours also offer a chance to meet people from all over the world. Shared experiences have a unique way of turning strangers into friends, even if only for a few hours. Ghost-themed tours are especially popular in a place like Las Vegas.

The Kings of Vegas: Mobsters and Casinos High roller Speakeasy Crawl takes you on a fascinating walking excursion through the Fremont Street district. You'll hear stories about the history and birth of Las Vegas and its mobster ancestry. This tour includes stops at bars along the way, including a speakeasy, adding to the authenticity. No mobster tour would be complete without an education on prohibition. This fun-filled tour costs between $24 and $29 and lasts around two hours.

The Vegas Ghosts: Gangsters, Glitz, and Gore Ghost Tour is a favorite for anyone who enjoys ghost stories, complete with hauntings and curses. This tour has no bar stops, but it offers plenty of thrilling stories that will make you say, "Oh my!"

3

Iconic Landmarks and Free Attractions

Iconic Landmarks and Free Attractions

It won't take long for you to be completely mesmerized by the sights and sounds of the Las Vegas Strip. As soon as your plane lands at the airport and you get a glimpse of it, the fascination begins. Getting from the airport to your hotel on the Strip is your first mini tour. If you choose to take a taxi or Uber and are lucky enough to get a chatty driver, you'll immediately experience your first guided tour. On a recent visit, our Uber driver was talkative and explained the changes made to the Strip in preparation for the Formula Race. He pointed out the grandstand being built in front of the famous Bellagio fountain, informing us that you can no longer stand on the Strip side of the sidewalk to watch the fountains due to the grandstand seating. Fortunately, we were staying at the Bellagio and had a view of the fountain from our room, so we didn't have to seek alternative ways to see the fountain shows.

Bellagio Conservatory & Botanical Gardens

After you've seen the Bellagio fountains do their thing, you might want to head inside to experience the Bellagio Conservatory & Botanical Gardens. The gardens change with the season, and I must say that for me, the winter holiday installation is my favorite, although it is magnificent during the spring and summer as well. This is a $0 experience that will be visually pleasing and make for great selfies or family pics. However, be aware it is a popular attraction, so if you plan to take photos with serious poses, you'll want to get there early before the crowds.

MGM's Leo the Lion

Another must-see on the Strip is MGM's Leo the Lion. This 45-foot bronze statue, installed in 1998, sits on a 25-foot pedestal and honors the lion that roars at the beginning of the MGM films. The original entrance for the MGM Grand Hotel and Casino featured a lion's head, but it was removed in 1997 because some Asian gamblers felt that walking into the lion's mouth was bad luck. So, the powers that be chose to remove the lion's head from the entrance and erect this magnificent must-see statue. This is a great spot to get some photos.

Fremont Street Experience

Then there's always the Fremont Street Experience. This pedestrian mall in downtown Las Vegas takes up over five blocks and is home to some of the city's most iconic hotels, such as Four Queens, Binion's, and Golden Nugget. There are moments at the Fremont Street Experience when you forget you are outside. There is so much to see and do; your head will be on a swivel with all that is going on. The Slotzilla Zipline experience is priced well above our $30 target, but just watching and listening to the brave souls enjoy the ride might be all you need. It is quite the spectacle. If you visit the Fremont Street Experience at night, you must get there in time to see the six to eight-minute largest light show in the world that starts around 6 PM and is completely free. You will be mesmerized!

4

Free and Cheap Strip Hotel Activities

Free and Cheap Strip Hotel Activities

STRAT Observation Tower & Thrill Rides

Looking for one of the most iconic, amazing views of the city and the Las Vegas Strip? Then you must visit the Stratosphere Hotel and Casino and ascend the tower for either the breathtaking Observation Tower or the Observation Tower and Thrill Rides. I can admit I'm not the thrill-seeking type, but I thoroughly enjoyed the view from the tower. For the more adventurous, there are two thrill rides:

- **Big Shot:** A ride that catapults you 160 feet (49 m) into the air.
- **X-Scream:** An amusement ride that dangles you 27 feet (8 m) off the tower's edge.

The prices for these observation activities are reasonable. For

$25, you can enjoy a view like no other in Las Vegas, and for an additional $4, you can add on the thrill rides if that's what your heart desires.

Note: There are height restrictions for the thrill rides:

- You must be at least 4 feet 3 inches (132 cm) tall to ride X-Scream or Insanity.
- You must be at least 4 feet (122 cm) tall to ride Big Shot.

Circus Circus Hotel and Casino

Circus Circus is the only casino with an actual circus inside. If you are traveling with kids, this is one of the best places for entertainment. Shows are on a schedule, so check with the hotel if you want to enjoy the show from beginning to end. It's quite a sight to walk through a casino and look up to see high-flying aerialists or trapeze artists performing awe-inspiring acts.

This hotel also features an arcade, the Adventuredome. In order to enjoy the rides in this theme park, a wristband will need to be purchased. They currently sell two types of wristbands: the Regular All-Day Ride Wristband for guests 48 inches and above for $60, and the Junior All-Day Ride Wristband for guests under 48 inches to 33 inches tall for $30. There is no age restriction. Admission to the park is free, but you need one of the wristbands to ride anything.

The Big Apple Coaster and Arcade at New York-New York Hotel & Casino

I am not a fan of roller coasters, but if you happen to be that thrill-seeking person, this roller coaster experience for about $25 is for you. Zip through the air at speeds of 70 mph while anticipating the 76-foot drops. When you're done with that, you can drop into the arcade and play a few games like Skee-ball,

Air Hockey, and NBA Fever.

Note: There is a height restriction for the roller coaster:

- Minimum height is 54 inches (137 cm) without footwear.

Shark Reef Aquarium & VR Experience Tickets at Mandalay Bay - $31

This activity is a smidge over our $30 limit, but I think that extra dollar will be worth it once you step inside this amazing aquarium. Get up close but not too personal with actual sharks behind very thick acrylic underwater viewing tunnels. This tunnel alone is worth the price of admission. Enjoy over 2,000 marine animals in 14 different exhibits with freshwater and saltwater fish and reptiles in temple-themed tanks. Other exhibits include a jungle setting and a sunken ship. Make sure you spend some time petting the stingrays.

The Las Vegas Strip High Roller Observation Wheel - $29

The wheel contains 28 cabins that take 30 minutes to complete one rotation and towers 550 feet above the center of the Strip. Catch the amazing view of Las Vegas from this ride at a not-so-high price of $29. I love it when great entertainment falls under our $30 target! Enjoy this option between 12 PM and 4:59 PM daily. The price goes up as the evening progresses, so don't miss this below-$30 window. Pro tip: buy your tickets early so you don't miss out!

Free or cheap live music and street performers

Just strolling down the strip or flying down Fremont street you are invariably going to experience a street performer.

Someone singing, dancing, entertaining in costume etc. The performers are required to register for a spot to perform, no guarantees there performances will be great but you can be sure to come across someone performing their hearts out to make you smile and maybe drop a dollar in their hat.

5

Hotel Lobbies

Hotel Lobbies

Some of the best free viewing is in hotel lobbies. We mentioned earlier about the lobby at the Bellagio with the gardens and the art installation in the ceiling of the lobby. This is just one of many lobbies that will make your jaw drop and your eyes bulge when you walk in.

The Venetian is full of art and sculptures that make you feel like you stepped off the Strip and right into Italy. The painted ceilings and the lighting are a key reason why you feel as though you have left Las Vegas and traveled abroad.

The Wynn is another must see. The vibrant decor and tiled floor make you instantly feel like you've walked into a garden instead of a hotel. This lobby could easily serve as a spot for reflection. It encourages you to slow down and appreciate what the beauty of this space has to offer.

The Paris hotel is another favorite. The Eiffel Tower is of course not nearly the size of the original in the beautiful city of

Paris but during the day it is an impressive site and at night it really shows its beauty as it is perfectly enhanced by the lighting. It is a must see if you are on the strip at night.

Every hotel on the Strip has a bar, and while they technically are not free, you can buy a drink and sit and enjoy some really good music in the evening. Paying for a drink in a bar is still cheaper than enjoying that same music while sitting at a slot machine or at the blackjack table.

6

Other Things to Do and See

Other Things to Do and See

Vegas Illuminated: 3-hour Ultimate Vegas Panoramic Night Bus Tour - $31
There is nothing like Las Vegas at night. This tour takes you on a journey where you experience the Las Vegas landmarks in all their illuminated glory. This is where true appreciation comes for the human genius behind the exterior glitz and glamour of the Strip. Experience the beauty of sites like the Bellagio, the MGM Grand, and Caesars Palace, which can only be seen and appreciated through the night sky. During the summer months, make sure to head to the top deck of the tour bus to get the absolute most out of the amazing night views of Las Vegas. This tour is about 3 hours and is a smidge over our $30 target at $31, but it is well worth the extra dollar, I promise.

The Neon Museum Las Vegas - $25
For this affordable price, you can plan a visit to the Neon

Museum during the day. Evening prices are a little higher, but the daytime visit is still worth the time and money. The history in this museum is unique, with the signs telling the stories that define what the city was, is, and will be.

As an added bonus, to encourage everyone to visit, the Museum for ALL program supports those receiving food assistance (SNAP) benefits with a minimal fee of $3.00 per person for up to four people.

Admission to the Erotic Heritage Museum Las Vegas $29

This next location I have not personally been to (yet), but I have had friends who have dared to venture to this museum, and they loved it. You will find everything from sculptures and mannequins to posters and magazine covers to educate yourself on the connection between art and sexuality that are older than the Renaissance. This museum houses more than 24,000 square feet of permanent and featured exhibits championing the wonders of erotic imagination, as depicted through artistic expressions of sex and love. Featured exhibits may change; however, one of the permanent exhibits is access to memorabilia from legendary guitarist and founder of the band Van Halen. The memorabilia in this exhibit is in the Catherine exhibit and features work Eddie Van Halen did on the film Sacred Sin. The price of this experience is $29.

Warning: This museum may not be suitable for anyone under the age of 18.

7

Outdoor Activities

Outdoor Activities

Less than 10 miles away from the Las Vegas Strip by car is a 68-acre sports park called Gary Reese Freedom Park. This park has plenty of open space and includes areas for basketball, softball, a skate park, horseshoe pits, volleyball courts, a walking/jogging path, playgrounds, barbecue grills, and a disc golf field, among other things. Reservations may be required for some activities, but if you just need to spend a day away from the crowds and lights of the Strip, this is the place to escape to.

During pool season in Las Vegas, which generally runs from March to October, one of the best free activities you can do is go to the pool. The hotel resort fees you pay allow you to access the pool at your hotel at no additional cost. Sure, you can spend money to get a cabana or reserve a pool chair, but that is only if you want to treat yourself to something special. Otherwise, the pools are an easy and free option. Some hotels offer public access for free or for a small fee. It is best to call any hotel you might be interested in to confirm their policy as things have a tendency to change, but in the past, the MGM would allow public access to their Grand Pool Complex. Also, check with your hotel if they are part of a brand such as MGM or Caesars—you may be able to visit pools at their other hotels for free. This will provide more options to enjoy, especially if you like to drift down a lazy river. Not every hotel has one, but the ones at the MGM and Mandalay Bay are pretty great.

8

Eating and Drinking

Eating and Drinking

We all know that meals and beverages in Las Vegas can be expensive, but let's take a look at some budget-friendly options. Lately, Las Vegas is offering something a little different than the basic food court. Food Halls are now popping up in Las Vegas hotels and casinos, inspired by foods from around the world. They are a little pricier than traditional food courts but indeed less expensive than some buffets or restaurants. These locations can satisfy your hunger for breakfast, lunch, or dinner.

Pro Tip: If you are eating at a food court or food hall linked to the hotel brand you are staying in, such as MGM or Caesars, make sure to charge your meal to your room. This will help build comps if you are also gambling at these properties. If gambling is not your thing, feel free to pay by your preferred method of cash, credit, or debit. Since COVID, most food halls or food courts are not open 24 hours a day, so please keep that in mind if you find a food court or hall you really want to try—it might not be a good idea to try them at 3 AM.

Food Halls:

- **Block 16 Urban Food Hall at The Cosmopolitan:** It is budget-friendly and offers options different from traditional burgers or pizza. Here you can find flatbread sandwiches, rice bowls, over 100 different donuts, espresso and coffee options, hot chicken, tequila and Mexican foods, and some Japanese cuisine.
- **Famous Foods Street Eats at Resorts World:** Inspired by Southeast Asia's street markets, come here for Michelin-recognized and award-winning dishes such as dumplings, handcrafted noodles, and rice dishes. Malaysian spice noodles and Hainanese chicken are also great options. You can also find American-inspired restaurants and world-inspired dishes like Nashville-style hot chicken, burgers, and gourmet pastries and sweets.
- **Proper Eats at Aria:** Here you will find a mix of styles, from Korean fried chicken and traditional Japanese sushi to a classic Jewish deli, burgers, and pizza. They have options for practically everyone.
- **The Food Hall at The Fremont Hotel in Downtown Las Vegas:** You can find familiar brands like Dunkin and Steak 'n Shake, but there are also new options. You'll find restaurants serving chicken tenders, sandwiches and wraps, rotisserie chicken and waffles, fried chicken, tacos, and fried rice. This location has it all at great prices.
- **Eataly at Park MGM:** Features a variety of Italian food that you can grab and go or sit down and enjoy. Although not technically a food hall or food court it operates in a

similar manner. Prices are not super cheap here but you will get your money's worth and your taste buds will thank you.

Food Courts:

- MGM Food Court: One of the best food courts in Las Vegas, offering options that make the budget-minded traveler happy. Here you can get food choices from New York to Hong Kong, including Nathan's Famous Hot Dogs, Johnny Rockets, Pan Asian Express, Tacos & Ritas, Original Chicken Tender, Häagen-Dazs, and Bonanno's New York Pizzeria. Make sure to check times as this location is not open 24 hours a day.
- Excalibur Food Court: In my opinion, it kicks up a notch from the MGM. They offer more choices, including Del Taco, Krispy Kreme Doughnuts, Cinnabon, Pizza Hut, Popeyes Chicken, Einstein Bagels, Fatburger, Pickup Stix (Asian Cuisine), Jimmy John's sandwiches, and Starbucks. Some of these locations will not be open 24 hours, so check and plan accordingly.
- **Fashion Show Food Court:** Offers more variety than the previous options. Here you can find The Habit Burger Grill, Ike's Love and Sandwiches, India Masala Cuisine, Opa! Of Greece, Panda Express, Philadelphia Steak & Hoagie, Suki Hana, and Villa Italian Kitchen.
- **The Village Eateries at New York-New York:** Offers Sirrico's New York pizza, sandwiches at Greenberg's Deli, fish and chips at Fulton's Fish Frye, fresh-baked pastries at the Village Bakery, and hot dogs at Times Square to Go.

9

Happy Hours and Drink Specials

Happy Hours and Drink Specials

Finding drink specials on the Strip that won't break the bank can be a challenge. Even some of the cheaper options we have covered are still not exactly "cheap." But our search continues to find the places that offer lower-cost spirits and food.

Downtown Cocktail Room (D.C.R.) boasts on its website that it is home to the best happy hour in Las Vegas. Happy Hour is Tuesday through Saturday from 5 PM to 8 PM and offers half off well and call spirits, beer, punch bowls, and wine, with $10 seasonal and classic cocktails.

The Parlour in downtown Las Vegas offers a "Pre-Inflation" menu on Thursday, Friday, and Saturday from 5:30 PM to 12 AM. They serve up smash burgers starting at $5 and crafted cocktails starting at $7! Check their website or Instagram for the latest updates.

El Segundo Sol at the Las Vegas Fashion Show Mall offers

Happy Hour Monday through Thursday from 3 PM to 6 PM. The offerings include bottomless chips and salsa and margaritas (on the rocks or frozen) for $6.50.

Fight Club located in the Venetian offers Happy Hour Monday through Friday from 4 PM to 6 PM. The selections include oysters in the half shell and shrimp cocktail for $1.50 each, four cheese flatbread and prime sliders for $10, Giesen and Matthew Fritz wine for $9 a glass, and Modelo draft beer for $6. Select happy hour cocktails, including Margarita, Cosmopolitan, Tom Collins, and Daiquiri, can be enjoyed for $10 each.

Shopping and Souvenirs

As you make your way up and down the Strip, you will find plenty of spots to stop and buy souvenir merchandise, both inside and outside the hotels and casinos. Buying souvenirs inside the hotels can be expensive, but if you want something authentically branded for that particular hotel, my suggestion is to buy your merch there. Otherwise, there are plenty of other places along the Strip or in downtown Las Vegas to find some lower-priced items to commemorate your Las Vegas experience.

Bonanza Gift Shop is one of your first stops for souvenir merch. With over 40,000 square feet of space, you are bound to find something you like. If nothing else, I love getting my calendars for the next year here.

Magnet Max in the Miracle Mile Shops is a must if you are a magnet lover like I am. Here you will find the perfect souvenir for friends and family and something for yourself to add to your refrigerator magnet collection of awesome places you have been.

The Grand Canal Shops at the Venetian is another great

stop for shopping. It is a little pricier than the other locations but offers a nice variety of items to choose from. Here you can find baby onesies, giant playing cards, and other Las Vegas-themed merch.

10

Tips and Tricks for Saving Money

Tips and Tricks for Saving Money

To help your dollar and our patience go farther while in Las Vegas, you will need to employ some tried and true tips and tricks to help make your trip the best it can be without breaking your bank or being driven to the edge of madness.

Travel During Off-Peak Times: Traveling in the earlier part of the day will result in fewer crowds and less aggravation, especially in the warmer months. To help with creating a breeze when it's excessively hot, bring along a small handheld personal fan to keep you cool when you aren't inside a building with air conditioning. One that mists you with water would be helpful but not required. Speaking of water, if you are in a casino and sitting at a machine, feel free to ask one of the servers for a bottle of water. They will happily provide one whether you are gambling or not. If you want something stronger than water, they will bring that also—give them a dollar or two for a tip as a courtesy. That is amazingly cheap for an alcoholic beverage that would have been ten times more if you went to the bar and got it yourself. I typically don't tip for water, but if you want to, it's perfectly okay.

Get a Players Card: Another neat tip is that if you are a gambler of any level, make sure you get the player's card for any casino you enter **before** you gamble one penny with them. These cards will help you earn points for comps on your next trip. Once you have the card, be sure to use it every single time you play a machine or table at a property linked to that card. The points add up and can easily help you get a few comped nights on your next visit or even a few dollars off your hotel bill. Make sure to charge your meals to your room if you are eating at a restaurant on one of the properties linked to your card. You never know how much your gambling spend could offset some of your meal costs.

Getting Around Free and Cheap: Some hotels have trams that carry you for free from one property to another. The MGM property has a tram with stops at Mandalay Bay, Excalibur, and Luxor. The Aria tram includes stops to access Park MGM, ARIA/Shops at Crystals, Vdara, and Bellagio.

The **Las Vegas Monorail** is not free but is a great option to help you navigate from one hotel and casino to another on the Strip. You could easily hop off the tram at the Bellagio and cross the street to catch the monorail to visit other properties. The Monorail runs a 3.9-mile route from the SAHARA Las Vegas Station to the MGM Grand Station. The seven stations on the route are:

- SAHARA Las Vegas Station
- Westgate Station

- Boingo Station at Las Vegas Convention Center
- Harrah's/The LINQ Station
- Flamingo/Caesars Palace Station
- Horseshoe/Paris Station
- MGM Grand Station

The Monorail offers a range of tickets from a single ride to a 7-day pass. Purchasing the ticket online will help you save a little more money than buying them at the station. The fares are subject to change, but starting on the website is the best way to get the current ticket prices. The prices will be lower than taking a couple of rideshares throughout the day and less hectic than trying to use the bus system, called the Deuce, only. The monorail will not have to sit in traffic, so consider its speed and convenience when planning your activities.

The Las Vegas Deuce is the bus system and easily accessible to ride up and down the Strip and beyond. For visitors the cost to travel can range from $4 for a single ride to $20 for a 3-day pass. Definitely a cheaper option than ride shares or taxis but if you choose this option make sure you are not in a hurry or are traveling off peak as these buses are easily slowed down by the traffic on the Strip.

11

Summary

As our journey through Las Vegas comes to an end, I hope this guide has opened your eyes to the numerous and varied budget-friendly activities the city offers beyond the glitzy casinos and high-stakes glamor. From the hidden gems on the Strip to the local spots known only to seasoned visitors, Las Vegas is a city brimming with affordable adventures waiting to be discovered.

We've walked the vibrant streets, explored iconic landmarks, and enjoyed spectacular free attractions. Whether you were mesmerized by the Bellagio fountains, enchanted by the art at The Venetian, or thrilled by the views from the STRAT Observation Tower, each experience was curated to give you the best of Las Vegas without breaking the bank.

We dined on a budget without compromising on flavor, enjoying diverse culinary delights at food halls like Block 16 Urban Food Hall and Proper Eats. And when the sun set, we discovered the best happy hours and drink specials, proving that great entertainment doesn't have to come with a hefty price tag.

Our excursions took us beyond the Strip as well. We basked in the tranquility of Gary Reese Freedom Park, floated down lazy rivers at hotel pools, and marveled at marine life at the Shark Reef Aquarium. We also delved into the vibrant nightlife with tours that showcased the illuminated beauty of Las Vegas at night.

In addition to fun and adventure, we shared tips and tricks for making the most of your trip, from utilizing players' cards to navigating the city with free trams and the efficient Monorail.

Please be sure to check out the references section for all the websites used to create this guide. Some may offer discounts if you go directly to their sites like the Monorail.

Las Vegas is more than just a gambler's paradise. It's a city full of surprises, waiting to be explored by both seasoned travelers and first-time visitors alike. Thank you for joining me on this budget-friendly adventure. May your future trips to Las Vegas be filled with unforgettable memories, new discoveries, and plenty of fun that won't break the bank. Safe travels, and happy exploring!

If you found this book helpful, I'd be very appreciative if you left a favorable review for the book on Amazon.

12

Resources

Art & Architecture | The Venetian Resort Las Vegas. (n.d.). https://www.venetianlasvegas.com/resort/attractions/art-and-architecture.html

Bellagio Hotel & Casino. (n.d.). https://bellagio.mgmresorts.com/en/entertainment/conservatory-botanical-garden.html

Coyle, M. (2024, November 5). *Sin City on a Budget: 8 ways to save on your next trip to Vegas.* NerdWallet. https://www.nerdwallet.com/article/travel/how-to-save-on-a-vegas-trip

Erotic Heritage Museum. (n.d.). https://www.eroticmuseumvegas.com/

Excalibur Hotel & Casino. (n.d.). https://excalibur.mgmresorts.com/en/restaurants/food-court.html

Experience, F. S. (2024, November 11). *Fremont street experience in downtown Las Vegas.* Fremont Street Experience. https://vegasexperience.com/?gad_source=1&gclid=Cj0KCQiAouG5BhDBARIsAOc08RTpPMQdoznNSWMcY7pOqDTdK

AKsI253AZe7W4BhFPkGEzoWfLGbf9caAgCgEALw_wcB

Free Circus acts at Circus Circus Las Vegas | Circus Circus Hotel & Casino Las Vegas. (n.d.). Circus Circus | Circus Circus Hotel & Casino Las Vegas. https://www.circuscircus.com/entertain ment-amenities-1/free-circus-acts/

Fremont Street Experience. (n.d.). Tripadvisor. Retrieved November 17, 2024, from https://www.tripadvisor.com/A ttraction_Review-g45963-d102514-Reviews-Fremont_Street _Experience-Las_Vegas_Nevada.html

Gary Reese Freedom Park. (n.d.). https://www.lasvegasnevada. gov/Residents/Parks-Facilities/Gary-Reese-Freedom-Park

Kirby, D., Smith, K., & Wilkins, M. (n.d.). *Las Vegas, Nevada: Leo The MGM Lion Statue*. Road Side America. Retrieved November 17, 2024, from https://www.roadsideamerica.com/ tip/40445#:~:text=Las%20Vegas%2C%20Nevada%3A%20Leo %20The,it%20would%20cause%20bad%20luck.

Mancini, A. (2024, August 30). From Buffets to Food Halls, the Latest Dining Trend in Vegas. *Neon Feast*. Retrieved November 17, 2024, from https://www.visitlasvegas.com/exp erience/post/from-buffets-to-food-halls-informal-dining-thri ves-in-las-vegas/

MGM Grand Las Vegas. (n.d.). https://mgmgrand.mgmresort s.com/en/restaurants/foodcourt.html

Mono-Admin. (2024, October 10). *Official route map of the Las Vegas monorail*. Las Vegas Monorail. https://www.lvmonor ail.com/route-map/

New York-New York Hotel & Casino. (n.d.). https://newyorkn ewyork.mgmresorts.com/en/entertainment/the-big-apple-co aster-and-arcade.html

Quezada, Z. (2019a, November 5). *Where to find food courts on the Las Vegas Strip*. TripSavvy. https://www.tripsavvy.com/f

ood-courts-on-las-vegas-strip-1678694

Quezada, Z. (2019b, November 5). *Where to find food courts on the Las Vegas Strip*. TripSavvy. https://www.tripsavvy.com/food-courts-on-las-vegas-strip-1678694

Shark Reef Aquarium & VR Experience tickets at Mandalay Bay. (2024, November 26). https://www.expedia.com/things-to-do/a.a183725.activity-details?&rid=178276&location=Las+Vegas+%28and+vicinity%29%2C+Nevada%2C+United+States+of+America&startDate=2024-11-26&endDate=2024-11-27&swp=off

Slattery, R. (2024, August 29). *Where to find the best happy Hour specials in Las Vegas*. Eater Vegas. https://vegas.eater.com/maps/best-happy-hours-las-vegas

STRAT Observation Tower & Thrill Rides. (2024, November 26). https://www.expedia.com/things-to-do/a.a449686.activity-details?&rid=178276&location=Las+Vegas+%28and+vicinity%29%2C+Nevada%2C+United+States+of+America&startDate=2024-11-26&endDate=2024-11-27&swp=of

The Las Vegas High Roller Wheel - the LINQ hotel. (n.d.-a). Caesars Home Page. https://www.caesars.com/linq/things-to-do/attractions/high-roller

The Las Vegas High Roller Wheel - the LINQ hotel. (n.d.-b). Caesars Home Page. https://www.caesars.com/linq/things-to-do/attractions/high-roller

The Neon Museum - we are the story of Las Vegas. (n.d.). The Neon Museum Las Vegas. https://neonmuseum.org/

Tripadvisor. (n.d.). *Kings of Vegas: Mobsters and Casinos Highroller Speakeasy Crawl*. Retrieved November 17, 2024, from https://www.tripadvisor.com/AttractionProductReview-g45963-d27504227-Kings_of_Vegas_Mobsters_and_Casinos_Highroller_Speakeasy_Crawl-Las_Vegas_Nevada.html

Vegas Illuminated: 3-hour Ultimate Vegas Panaromic Night Bus Tour. (2024, November 26). https://www.expedia.com/things-to-do/a.a49431697.activity-details?&rid=178276&location=Las+Vegas+%28and+vicinity%29%2C+Nevada%2C+United+States+of+America&startDate=2024-11-26&endDate=2024-11-27&swp=off

Ways to Travel Fares & Passes. (n.d.). RTC. Retrieved November 17, 2024, from https://www.rtcsnv.com/ways-to-travel/fares-passes/

Williamson. (2024, January 25). 10 best Souvenir shops in Las Vegas. **Vegas Always. https://www.vegasalways.com/las-vegas-souvenir-shops/**